How to Stop Hating Your Ex…

so you can co-parent in peace

By René Ashton

Abundant
Media

I'm happy to donate a
portion of this book's sales
to the
MAKE A WISH
FOUNDATION.

DEDICATED TO
OLIVIA, OWEN AND EMMA

Special quantity discounts
for bulk purchases for sales,
promotions, fundraising, or
educational use.

QUESTION FOR YOU. YES, YOU, READER!

Why did you pick up this book? (Or why are you scrolling through the pages online?)

Are you thinking, "Yeah, why am *I* reading this? My stupid, bleep-bleeping ex should be reading this! He did this bullsh*t thing and pulled that bullsh*t thing and he…" It could feasibly go on and on, right? Well, if you want to change the way you feel, act and react to your ex, read on but I've got to tell you now, this book isn't only going to be about your ex, it's going to be about you.

I wrote this book because I had a dire need to read it, and I could not find anything similar to it out there. Unlike most of the self improvement books available, mine tells you much of my own story. The reason I found it necessary to do this was because there were numerous times I went searching the aisles of my local bookstores in hopes of finding someone's story like mine. I wanted to hear far worse stories than mine in hopes that maybe, just maybe, it would make me feel better and help put things in perspective. I had no perspective. I had hatred (a lot). I wanted desperately to know that I was not alone. I wanted someone to tell me how in the world I was to escape the grips of this ferocious animal wreaking havoc in my life, my anger.

"At last an amazing book has arrived, *How To Stop Hating Your Ex So You Can Co-Parent in Peace*. This information will provide millions of parents with an educational tool that will teach, motivate, test, solve and change barriers that often interfere with the important task of parents working together after a divorce or separation.

René Ashton's personal experiences of struggling and surviving are comforting and insightful. Ms. Ashton encourages one to become transparent with their own emotions without guilt as they work through the difficult process of parenting after a separation.

A valuable resource long passed due. Thanks."

~Jacqueline Bunkley~Social Worker, Teacher &
Consultant/ Guest Lecturer for the Los Angeles
Superior   Court/ Family Court Services/ PACT

"Overcoming abusive relationships is a multi-dynamic process. René Ashton's book kick-starts the healing by compassionately bringing the reader to a safe place to examine his/her own needs and the strengths possessed to achieve them."

~Julia P. Pengra Clarke, M.A. RDT

"*How to Stop Hating Your Ex So You Can Co-Parent in Peace* is a masterpiece. Not only does René share her personal life story and her many challenges, she also mentors and encourages you throughout the book with tips and tools to support you when dealing with your ex. What a powerful combination!"

~Joanie Winberg, Founder and CEO National Association of Divorce for Women & Children~NADWC.org

"René's book is a brilliant and down to earth reminder that our children and our joy must be priorities, that forgiveness is so important and powerful, and that world peace begins at home."

~Wendy Spiller, Spiritual Coach LifeLovesYou.ws

"An honest look at taking responsibility for yourself and moving out of the victim place and into personal power, this book shows you how with humor blended with the tears."

~Jean Adrienne, Author & Internet Talk Show Host of Inner-Speak.com

"This book offers a unique combination of a personal story and thought provoking suggestions and exercises. Although the topic of divorce and co-parenting is laden with theory and deep emotions, René's casual and humorous writing style makes it an easy read. While validating the overwhelming emotions (so important!) which arise as a result of divorce and co-parenting issues, René's analogies and metaphors elicit the recognition reflex and an occasional chuckle (also very important!). 'There was a lot of water loss in my body during the pregnancy. It all came from my eyes!' I like the way she reinforced and repeated the significance of working through the exercises, which provide a valuable tool for insight, awareness and eventual healing.

How to Stop Hating Your Ex So You Can Co-Parent in Peace reveals that it isn't just about "going" through but rather "growing" through the difficult life experience of divorce and co-parenting. Just as René did, readers will be able to acquire insight and awareness in order to emerge as whole and happy people who are excellent parents and positive role models for their children".

~Linda A. Lucatorto, M.Ed., CPC
OasisExperience.com

"Are you spending every waking hour hating your ex for the misery in your life? Many people feel this way after divorce. I hear from women all the time who are still angry at their ex many years after their divorce. This is such a waste because this resentment keeps them chained to the past, unable to move on and enjoy life. Do you really want to be controlled by your bitter feelings ten years from now?

If you're ready to move on with your life, then take the time to read *How to Stop Hating Your Ex So You Can Co-Parent in Peace* by René Ashton. This is a great book for any parent who is struggling with their feelings about co-parenting with an ex that has caused them pain.

Using her own trials and tribulations as an example, René walks you through the steps to peel back the layers of anger, hurt, and resentment that may be holding you back from being the best parent for your child. This is a hands-on; roll up your sleeves type of book that requires more than just casual reading (which is often quickly forgotten). With guided exercises, you can begin to work through your emotions and get past the bitterness that colors your world. And yes, it really is possible.

Even though the book is geared towards helping you co-parent in peace, it's also an excellent resource for helping anyone move past a break-up, separation, or divorce. By taking control of how you feel about the situation, you can then focus on becoming the best parent for your child. And after all, that's what it's all about."

~Tracy Achen, Founder of WomansDivorce.com

"As a mediator, I have conducted well over 4,500 child custody mediations. Many disputed issues can be avoided, making court intervention unnecessary if divorcing parents learn how to deal with their own thoughts and emotions first. *How to Stop Hating Your Ex* lays out a very simple, yet effective way to do just that and as a result, save themselves and their children a lot of heartache.

I heartily endorse René Ashton's work because she speaks truth straight from her own experiences. I am convinced that if more post-divorce parents would apply what she teaches, there would be fewer protracted family law court cases and families would be able to get on with their lives much sooner."

~Richard E. Abbey, MA
Empowering Families
Ventura, CA
EmpowerMyFamily.com

"How to Stop Hating your Ex so you can Co-Parent in Peace is more than just a book; it's a tool single parents can use to help achieve co-parenting success.

Although the divorce process is hard enough for people to face, trying to adjust to life after divorce is more difficult than many realize. Throwing children into the mix can potentially lead to a disaster if parents aren't prepared for the challenges presented while parenting with an ex.

René Ashton's book helps readers take the focus off hating an ex-spouse and put the focus on themselves and what they can control. Learn what you can do to take control of a situation right along with the author. Put the focus back on you and what you can do to be more productive while completing the exercises in the book along with the author.

This book is a great way to get down to business and figure out how you really feel about the situations you face, your ex and yourself. But more importantly, the book will help you work through those feelings so you can make having a successful parenting relationship with your ex achievable and triumphant.

After divorce, make sure your child knows you are there for him or her. Get helpful tips on how to choose activities that will be fun for you and your child. The book does a great job at getting readers to think about themselves for a change, as well as how to create the best environment for their child.

Realize with the help of this book that you aren't in a relationship with your ex anymore. Stop yourself from continuing to be the relationship you once had – take a breath and get your power back after reading Ashton's section about past relationships.

Wake up and smell the coffee! This book even points out how the emotions you have been bottling up inside are affecting your body.

René Ashton does a wonderful job relating to the feelings and situations her readers are experiencing while co-parenting. She helps readers learn from her mistakes and grow by looking at their actions.

All-in-all How to Stop Hating your Ex so you can Co-Parent in Peace is a quick yet informative read that offers readers a look at how successful co-parenting can work. René's easy-going tone makes it feel like you are having a conversation with a friend rather than reading a How-to book.

~Erin Kelley
Writer for Total Divorce

Whatever the mind of man can conceive and believe it can achieve.
Napoleon Hill

Foreword

High conflict divorce continues to produce terrible and sometimes lifelong psychological damage to the children of divorce. One of the most challenging obstacles for parents to overcome are decisions revolving around custody schedules and post-divorce co-parenting. Custody decision-making is a notorious battleground with the quest being "to win" child custody. Sadly, there really are no winners during a divorce and the losers in this battle are always the children. Parents lose sight of the fact that the person they are battling with is the mother or father of their child and that child only wants to see and hear about the good in each parent. Focusing on the ex-spouse tends to blind parents from the insight and awareness of the harm they are causing their children by arguing, fighting, and being vicious in front of the eyes and ears of their own children.

In my practice I coach parents how to get through a divorce or custody dispute on the path of least resistance. Eventually, there is almost always a sense of relief by my clients that they no longer have to fight, but instead can advocate with purpose and good child-centered judgment. This is an uphill effort, but the parents who stick with it are the ones willing to do the personal work that requires them to keep their children's best interests in the forefront. This orients a parent to a personal and internal therapeutic undertaking rather than an external battle that has collateral damage to the child. Growth does not come with easy decisions, but always with personal change and substantial compromise to be the better person and better parent.

How to Stop Hating Your Ex, So You Can Co-Parent in Peace comes as a valuable resource for any parent going through a divorce. I have found it to be extremely unique in the brutal honesty that was disclosed by René Ashton's journey through a painful co-parenting relationship and custody matter. If you are a parent in a divorce, you will surely identify with her regardless of your gender and learn from her shared strengths and weaknesses. The exercises in this book are ones that promote your own honesty and encourage you to remain engaged in prioritizing your child's needs. It will hold you accountable for being responsive to their development and well being. This accountability can raise your esteem and challenge you to reach your potential to be an optimal role model as the mother or father your child deserves. This book will become a "must-read" and "must-do" form of therapeutic homework for the clients in my practice in years to come.

Dr. Eric Frazer,
Forensic Psychologist, Assistant Clinical Professor-
Yale University School of Medicine
www.drfrazer.com

My story.
I've been a single parent since inception and now, years later share 50/50 custody. Here's what happened…I've gone from DESPISING my ex's every word to inviting him and his wife and mother-in-law over for BBQ's *and* sharing holidays. Nicely.

Prepare to qualify.
Time to take a serious look at where you are and where you want to be regarding your relationship with your ex.

Feelings…wo, wo, wo, feelings.
You have to acknowledge your feelings AND deal with them to move forward, so let's get to work.

Just curious.
They say, "Curiosity killed the cat." What if, in this case, *your* case, it HEALED the cat?" Let's take some inventory and see what we come up with.

You are not your relationship with your ex.
Do you have any idea what this means? If someone casually asks, "How are you?" and you dump a gripe

about your ex, you have BECOME that relationship.

shared visit…for the sake of YOUR KIDS! This isn't about you.

Chapter 11 page 157
Are you a statistic?
Studies show that 41% of divorced people 10 years later STILL hate their ex.* Do you really want to be a statistic? Do you really want to do that to *your* child? It's *your* choice.

Chapter 12 page 163
In closing.
I'm so grateful that you choose to pick up this book, read it cover to cover, participate it the exercises, acknowledge your part and create a healthy living environment for you and your child. Not only are they the better for it, so are you! I applaud you!

*Constance Ahrons's book, "The Good Divorce"

I feel the need for a disclaimer.

Disclaimer

I am not a licensed psychotherapist, or a child development specialist or a marriage and family counselor. I am a single mom who came from a divorced home and I have spent numerous hours with those professionals listed above seeking help for myself. What you are about to read is how I got through the process of hating my ex. I personally like how-to books and I couldn't find one specifically on this subject, so I decided to figure it out myself and write about it along the way. If any portion of this book helps you in any way, shape or form, I am grateful.

Okay, having said that, I feel the need for one more disclaimer.

Disclaimer 2

Since I am a female and my ex is a male, I am going to use the pronoun "he" in reference to ones "ex." Do I think that males are the source of all problems in relationships? Absolutely not! I want to be very clear about that. So, men, please do not take offense. Know that there will be stories in here about crazy making female ex's as well, and I will use the word "she" in telling those men's escapades. But first, here's my story.

Chapter 1

My Story

I was thirty one years old and still hopeful of finding the man of my dreams, riding off into the sunset and making babies with Mr. Right. Mr. Right, Mr. Right-Now, I got confused between the two. In hindsight I wasn't really confused, I wanted to be loved and I thought that I was. They say "love is blind" but I've come to determine that love itself is not blind. Love is a beautiful, magical gift we all crave to experience. The "blind" reference in the saying is what we *choose* to see when we are in love. Or should I say choose NOT to see. Ironically, if I had enough self esteem at that time to see the red flags my ex was physically holding in each hand and waving frantically in front of my face, I would probably be without the greatest joy in my life, my daughter.

We dated for a grand total of ten months, broke up (mutually), and two weeks later we decided to meet for lunch. As I ordered a milkshake to accompany my chicken noodle soup, bagel, bacon and eggs, my ex commented that my breasts looked larger. Well, yeah, I was pre-menstrual. It just so happened that in those two weeks New Years Eve had passed so, of course, as a mature adult (or not) I puked January 1st due to excessive drinking, I assumed. Oh, and once the day after for good measure. Not a common occurrence, by any stretch, but easily justified by the excessive holiday festivities. Then he uttered those three little words. Unfortunately, they weren't "I love you", but "Are you pregnant?" Although, I didn't think he was funny, in that moment I did think it could possibly, maybe, oh my God, be true. Within two hours of our lunch, I had gone to my local drug store, purchased a pregnancy test, peed on the little stick as directed and called him to make idle chatter as I waited to see if the little pink line would appear. Not only did it appear, it turned almost purple as if to say "Hello, you are definitely pregnant. No mistaking it. You're having a baby. Congratulations and good luck to you". Sure enough, eight pregnancy tests later, one confirmed by my doctor, I acknowledged that I was indeed with child.

Much to my amazement, my ex was thrilled with the idea of being a father and "Of course, let's be back together." We had one fabulous month of excitement, picking names, spending almost every night together, talking incessantly about "our" baby and planning his or her life. Until…well, he decided that he wanted nothing to do with me. Not something you tell a pregnant female whose hormones are raging! At this point I had already seen the heart beat on an ultra sound and was madly in love with him or her.

I was devastated. Heartbroken and devastated. He was very clear that we were over and would never be a couple again. I too was very clear that I was having this child with or without him. It was a very difficult, very emotional eight months filled with promises made and broken by the ex. Whether or not my feelings were valid, I hated, loathed and despised him with a fervor that took up entirely too much energy. It took an inordinate amount of effort, love and support from my amazing friends and family to get me through that very rough time. But I did. And as much as I hated him, there wasn't a day that I didn't want him to realize that he loved me and wanted to be with me. Pathetic? Yes. True? Unfortunately.

It never happened. There was no love on his part and he again made it clear that there would never be. Having said that, I, of course, was still convinced that he was just scared and surely he would come around. Silly me. Hopeful me.

During this time, he approached me with one of the cruelest things imaginable. Now, in the first draft of my book, as I was figuring out how NOT to hate my ex, I wrote about this event and many other unkind, confusing, and inappropriate things he did. Since this book is not meant as a vehicle to bash him, I no longer despise him, and my daughter now knows about this book, I will only share the least offensive things possible.

As the painful experiences continued, I attempted to release my sadness, frustration and anxiety by writing it all in a letter. I somehow thought if I reminded him of all the promises he made and broke, he would miraculously see the error of his ways and apologize. As I pulled up to his place to leave the letter, he arrived at that exact moment with his new girlfriend. It was as if the world had suddenly started to move in slow motion.

I could physically feel my heart ache. Really, my heart ached, my head spun, I felt dizzy, I felt as if I could no longer be in my own skin I hurt so badly. I felt so out of control and the worst part was I felt like the panic attack I was experiencing would do damage to my unborn child. Ugh! The sadness. The anger.

There was a lot of water loss in my body during the pregnancy. It all came from my eyes. Having said that, I was also very, very lucky to have an amazing support group of friends and family. At one point my apartment was so cluttered with second hand baby paraphernalia and gifts from loved ones, I thought to myself, I suppose people feeling sorry for me has one advantage. I didn't have to purchase much to prepare for the arrival of the most adorable child to walk this earth. Years later I realized they didn't feel sorry for me; they needed to get rid of their baby stuff to make room for their toddler stuff. There's so much stuff involved with having children, right?

I continued to include my ex in every aspect of the pregnancy hoping that he would somehow magically become interested. More foolish efforts. Yet, I tried none-the-less.

Like so many women, I thought I could change him. I could be that one "special one." It sounds so cliché and textbook, but it was unfortunately my reality. I was convinced that he could not, NOT be in love with me. How was it possible? I was carrying *his* child and I was growing a miracle inside me. Me. A miracle. For those of you mothers out there, I know you understand.

At the time, my mind was not clear enough to heed my therapist's advice to accept my reality and act accordingly. I wanted love from this particular person and of course, the more I wanted it, the more it pushed him away.

I wish I could say that was the end of the heart ache, but it continued every single solitary day until our daughter was about two years old. Yes, two. Painstakingly, I finally started to realize that it was never going to happen between us and I had better start letting go if I was ever going to move on. It was not easy. It was not pleasant. It was so very difficult to let him come over almost every day to love, adore and dote on this precious little girl and not me.

Despite the nasty, spiteful things he did and said, to be totally honest with you, there were still fleeting *moments*, I highlight *moments* because I like to acknowledge that they were only *moments* as opposed to months, which I continued to hope to unite our family for the next year. Embarrassing? Yes. Honest? Yes.

For the first three years of my daughter's life, the relationship I had with her father was very difficult. It was difficult because I hated him or difficult because I thought I loved him. I know there's the catch phrase, "Time heals all wounds", but the fact of the matter was, I didn't have the time to wait for that to happen. I couldn't live in hatred a moment longer. I didn't want to be one of those mothers who bad mouths a child's father in front of the child or in even their ear shot. It can be very difficult to reverse the damage your fighting parents can create. I know.

My parents' relationship was straight from a soap opera. If you think those daytime dramas are far-fetched, unfortunately, you're wrong. They fought, they cheated, they yelled, they screamed, they threw things; they stuck their tongues out at each other when exchanging us kids. Truly unbelievable. And the worst part was they included us in all of the drama. I don't mean they just yelled at each other in front of us, my dad would finish the fight, call my mom the "C" word, and then tell me "I hate your mother." And if that weren't bad enough, he would follow it up with, "You look just like her" and walk away. Now, my mom wasn't up for "parent of the year" award either. She would take me in the car and make me ride with her, following my dad to his latest secretary's house so we could catch him having an affair. And yes, he usually was. I don't even know how many times I packed his bags myself with the hopes that he would move out for good and they would stop fighting. Did I mention the years of therapy I've been through?

It has taken me a lot of painstaking work to deal with my past, accept my present and create a new future. It has been at times unbelievably overwhelming, sad, painful and lonely. To keep my daughter from experiencing what I did, I had to repeatedly make conscious choices to provide the best possible situation for her, and that meant getting along with her dad. Like it or not. (Mostly, I did *not* like it by the way.) I didn't (and don't) deal so well with functioning in a state of anxiety from constant fighting. Who does?

You may be reading this thinking, "Please, her story is nothing. My rat bastard ex cheated on me with my own sister and knocked her up, now they're living together." Or, "Well, I had to get a restraining order against my ex for spousal abuse." Or, "That's nothing, my ex is a drug addict and won't pay child support and doesn't even want to see his child." Yes, there are many more devastating situations than mine, yet we all feel that gut wrenching black hole of pain. It can be at times unbearably painful to even exist.

There are times when we want to hurt the other person emotionally and make them feel as horrible as we do. Although that may prove to provide some very satisfying moments of revenge, in the long run it will get us nowhere and only hurt our children in the process.

I had the power to change my situation, you do to.

Change begins with you.

Chapter 2

Prepare to Qualify

I'm assuming that you're reading this book because you're not in such a great place with your ex and are having a hard time dealing with your current situation. So, let's get to work.

I'm going to take you through all the steps I went through to get me to a peaceful place of co-parenting.

First, I suggest that you actually use this book as a tool to change your situation, and that means REALLY doing the writing exercises. Even if you're clear that you already know the answer and don't feel the need to write it down, you will be surprised how much more will come out of you if you actually put your pen to the page.

I suggest that when writing your answers, write without punctuation. Write without capitol letters. Write without periods. Leave out commas, parentheses, etc… Write with absolutely no restrictions. It's amazing how writing in this fashion can keep you from being left brained, allowing a stream of consciousness to take over, giving you more potential to express thoughts or feelings you may not have even realized you had.

You!

Here's your first question and you need to answer this honestly to get anything out of this book. Do *you* want to change? If you're thinking "Of course I want *him* to change!" That is not what I asked. You cannot change your ex. Let me say that again, you cannot change your ex. Try as you may. Manipulate as you may. Punish, kick, scream, whatever your tactic, it won't work. The only thing you can change is *yourself* to make things different. It sounds cliché, but it's true. Do not enter into this endeavor with the hopes of him magically turning a new leaf. Remember that this is for you, for your sanity, your health and your wellbeing. I'll remind you of that along the way.

So, I ask you again, do *you* want to change? When you answer this, please do not just put yes or no. Write yes or no and then write why. What will it do for you? How will it change you? What would you like to get out of it? You may not even be aware that you *don't* want to change. You may not like the situation you're in, but you actually may be comfortable *not* getting along with him. You may think that it will make you look weak if he did something terrible to cause the split and now here you are getting along as if nothing happened. I know one woman who secretly didn't want to get along with her ex because she said if she did; it would be letting him off the hook for cheating. You too may actually enjoy the drama. Yes, you heard me. You just might. It might make you feel alive. It might make you feel comfortable or safe. You may not know anything else so you may have fear or resistance to living any other way and believe me, there is another way.

Before you start writing, I want you to make sure that you do not write about *him*, how you want *him* to change. If you do that, I want you to take your pen, cross it out and write about YOU! You, you, you. This book is for you.

Here's my example.

- **Do you want to change?**

of course i want to change that seems like such a stupid question to ask myself why wouldn't i want to change i want to get along with him what could possibly be bad about that situation (insert long pause here) *oh my god* (insert tears here) *i'm afraid that if I get along with him i will like him again and want to be with him and it's taken me so long to get over the idea of not being with him shit shit fuck piss what is wrong with me how can i get along with him and not want to be with him why does this seem so hard uugghhh*

So, go ahead. Write your answer to the following question:

- **Do you want to change?**

I absolutely want to change for I know I haven't kept my side of street altogether clean I know my faults and I know my weaknesses and the pain that my actions have caused I've come to the conclusion that my changes need to come from within, they aren't solely for the good of our child but also for the good of my soul and spirit

Im fully aware that although I'm only half of the equation my part of the equation was detrimental to all involved. I want to change many things in my life as we all do so I will go about it one step at a time. I want to love my daughter as I always have, and I want nothing to get in the way of that. Each day I wake up and follow the buddhist path I recently been shown and will continue to do so until change is relevant.

If you wrap your emotional life around the weakness of another person, you have empowered those weaknesses to control you.
Unknown

Good work on the writing and being excruciatingly honest. Now...

WHAT'S YOUR PART?

There was a stretch of time where I literally spent every moment of every day HATING my ex. First of all, what a waste of energy. Second, it wasn't good for my health, mentally or physically. Third, my hating him, gave *him* the power. And, lastly, I was contributing to the vicious cycle of fighting that we were in. That was hard to admit, that I had anything to do with him acting the way he did. It wasn't that I did or said the same awful things that he did; it was that I was allowing it to continue to happen, by reacting the same way every time.

I read a fabulous quote in the book by Peter McWilliams, "Do It! Let's Get Off Our Buts" that said, "If you do what you've always done, you'll get what you've always gotten." *I* was fueling the fire with hatred. The worst part of all of this was, how could I possibly hate someone I didn't care about? Think about it? If you walked by a homeless person on the street and he hurled some derogatory remark at you, there's a good chance you'd look him in the eye, think he was crazy and continue walking. You may not even look back to give him any justification of getting your goad, because you weren't "gotten." He had no effect on you because you did not care about him. What I'm saying here is, it may be time for you to do some serious inventory on *yourself*.

So, I'm sure you're very clear on *his* part in your hatred toward him, but I want you to identify *your* part. Yes, you. What's your part in this?

Admitting your wrongdoing to yourself is a huge step. Admitting it to him is just as big. Is it necessary? No. Do I recommend it? That is something only you can decide. The fact that you acknowledge your participation and forgive yourself for it just may be enough for you.

If you do admit your part to him, please do not expect a "thank you" afterward. Do not expect for him to admit *his* wrongdoings. And don't do what I did, expect him to instantly change. He is who he is. This is for you. Will it make you feel better to tell him? Again, that is for you to decide. For me, I always need to get everything off my chest. Was I frustrated afterward? Only when I expected a response I didn't get. Don't expect anything!!!

If you so choose to accept this mission and tell him, remember that doing this is for you and only you. And for the love of Pete, don't include his wrongdoings in your admittance. The point of this book is to end the fighting, not create more of it.

When you are truly capable of acknowledging your part of this chaos, then and only then will you have a good shot at diminishing it. It may not sound fair to you if *he* was the one who cheated, if *he* was the one who left, if *he*... But somehow, someway you have or are contributing to the unpleasant situation you are in. When you own up to your own negativity, take responsibility for it, you will inevitably feel relief at some point. To let yourself off the hook for harboring ill will is liberating. It gives you a sense of self. Self worth, mainly. You will start to see a potential for change. I promise. It may not come instantly, but if you're looking to stop functioning in a world of anxiety, bitterness, hatred and dysfunction, this will bring you results. *You* will bring you results.

So, what have you done negatively to contribute to this situation that you are in? Come on, you're no angel. Fess up and use as many pages as needed to honestly answer this question. Make no excuses, post no blame, just be real with yourself and admit to your contributions.

Here's ONE of my examples. (I admit it; I was certainly a contributor, if not an instigator in many of our ugly scenarios.)

- **What have you done negatively to contribute to the situation you're experiencing?**

sometimes i jump to conclusions but he set it up that way when he did fucking mean things that i now anticipate him doing now fine whatever i'm not doing the exercise right but he should be doing this not me what was the question again what have i done blah blah blah i do anticipate his crappy cold callous behavior and i guess i shouldn't cause i really don't know what anyones ever gonna do until they do it

Your turn.

- **What have you done negatively to contribute to the situation you're experiencing?**

_____

_____

_____

_____

_____

_____

_____

_____

_____

_____

_____

_____

_____

_____

_____

This above all: To thine own self be true and it must follow as the night and the day thou cans't not then be false to any man. William Shakespeare

_____

Good work.

Now, I know I already said it, but I must say it again, just because *you* are doing the work and making changes on the inside, don't expect him to be changing right along with you. You'll set yourself up for frustration. I know.

I would get so frustrated at my ex. I would actually think, "How could he possibly not see my efforts, appreciate them, or much less acknowledge them with a "Thank you for accommodating your schedule for my every whim." Silly me. I found myself getting frustrated often and wanted to just say "Hi, let me keep making an effort, adjusting my schedule for you and you just keep walking all over me. I'm a doormat, it's okay." It seemed as if I were getting nowhere.

The thing was - I *was* getting nowhere. It was counter-productive to consciously make choices to react differently to him and then be pissed off that he was not following suit. I set up false expectations for myself that if I changed, he would change as well.

Now, is this some magic exercise that once you admit your wrongdoings, things will just instantly change? No, sorry. It's a first step. Without awareness, there can be no change. Will you still find some of his actions rude, inappropriate, vile or just plain irritating?

Maybe. Will you still have moments where you get unbelievably mad at something he did or said? Could very well be. But choose to make them moments, not days or weeks or years and remember that no matter how small, you had some part in all of this as well.

Make the choice to respond differently for you. For your inner peace. It will not come from him or any other outside source. It comes from you.

FORGIVE YOURSELF.

Now that you've acknowledged your part in this madness, I want you to forgive yourself for your contribution. And yes, that means writing it down.

Okay, here's one of my examples.

- **I forgive myself for...**

    i forgive myself for sleeping with a man who admittedly always pictured himself having children but not actually being with the kids mother i forgive myself for knowing what he wanted but continuing to date him knowing that i pictured it all happening another way

Yeah, don't think I wasn't mad at myself for a very, very long time.

Now it's your turn. Write away.

- **I forgive myself for...**

_____

_____

_____

_____

_____

_____

_____

_____

_____

_____

_____

_____

_____

_____

_____

_____

_____

_____

_____

_____

_____

_____

_____

Did you write it all down? If not, this great quote by Will Rogers is for you, "Even if you're on the right track, you'll get run over if you just sit there."

You're on the right track!!! So write, my friend, write.

You are worthy of forgiveness. Strong people forgive. Weak people accuse.

Chapter 3

Feelings, wo, wo, wo, feelings.

HOW DO YOU FEEL ABOUT YOUR EX?

And saying that you hate him does not qualify as an answer for our purposes. If your first thoughts are "He did *this* awful thing and said *that* dreadful thing and he's a miserable human being and he's just trying to punish me and blah, blah, blah." The list could justifiably go on forever, but those are not feelings.

Are you angry with him? Are you sad? Do you feel abandoned by him? Do you feel used by him? Do you feel jealous? Unacknowledged, unresolved feelings within you are certain to cause internal conflict resulting in external conflict. We don't want more of that.

As easy as it is, please do not get caught up in writing about what "he" has done, it is not important in this moment. Let's focus on you. Be specific about your feelings. They may be illogical and confusing to even you. They don't need to make sense right now. Just get them out.

You cannot heal what you cannot feel. I know that sounds cliché, but it is so true. You must move through your feelings; not around them, or over them, or under them, but through them. And in case you were wondering, you can't shop them away. I tried. You just can't move through them unless you acknowledge them. Besides, it will be almost impossible to experience new, healthy, loving feelings for yourself or someone else until you acknowledge what is going on right now.

Be honest and be very specific. Don't edit yourself. There is no right or wrong. No one is judging you, including you. Did your inner critic hear that? No judging yourself. Stay out of your own way and express your truth at this present moment.

Here's my example.

- **How do you feel about your ex?**

  i feel jealous every time he hugs and kisses my daughter i hate it it makes my skin crawl it makes me want to cry

So, how do you feel about him? Don't stop until you get it all out. But first read this eloquent excerpt from Elia Kazan's book, "A Life."

"Speak now, I said to myself, release your true feelings before it's too late. Be yourself. Take your place in the world. You are not a cosmic orphan. You have no reason to be timid. Respond as you feel. Awkwardly, crudely, vulgarly, but respond. Leave your throat open. You can have anything the world has to offer, but the thing you need most and perhaps want the most is to be yourself. Stop being anonymous. The anonymity you believed would protect you from pain and humiliation, shame and rejection, doesn't work. Admit rejection, admit pain, admit frustration, admit pettiness, even that, admit shame, admit outrage, admit anything and everything that happens to you. Respond with your true, uncalculated response, your emotions. The best and most human parts of you are those that you've inhibited and hidden from the world. Notice how in your past- every time you were angry, you were frightened. You have a right to anger. You don't have to earn it. Take it. Express it. Anger saves."

Write away.

- **How do you feel about your ex?**

_____

_____

_____

Good work.

Now…

HOW DO YOU FEEL ABOUT HOW YOU FEEL?

Really. Are you hard on yourself for still loving him? Are you angry with yourself for the uncontrollable jealousy? Do you feel guilty that you wish ill will upon him? Without thinking about it, write how you feel about how you feel. You can always tear these pages out and burn them when you are through. Just get it out.

Here is my example.

- **How do you feel about how you feel?**

  i feel bad that i'm jealous i feel like a bad person why wouldn't i want my daughter to have love and affection from her own father i'm sad because i want it for me i'm jealous of an infant that must make me a bad person loser how pathetic am i

Your turn.

- **How do you feel about how you feel?**

_____

_____

_____

_____

_____

_____

_____

_____

_____

_____

_____

_____

_____

_____

_____

_____

_____

_____

_____

_____

_____

_____

_____

Now that you've acknowledged your feelings about how you feel, it is important to-

FORGIVE YOURSELF.

Right, wrong, good, bad or indifferent, you deserve to feel however it is that you do. Your friends, his friends, your therapist, or your parents, may not agree with or support how you feel, but I want you to take a minute and honor your feelings. You need to be compassionate with yourself to move through this phase. You have to give yourself permission to feel hurt, sad, lonely, disappointed, pathetic or whatever else it is whether it makes sense or not. Now, here's an odd thing, you may have found yourself feeling love, desire or passion along with those negative feelings as well, and that's okay too.

If you're anything like me, I was kicking myself for letting him get to me like he did and that only made matters worse. Not only was I mad at him for these feelings, I was mad at myself for feeling them.

I want you to forgive yourself for feeling however you do toward him. Yes, you forgive you. Go ahead, tell yourself that it is okay by taking each feeling and forgive yourself for them. Please don't skip this. It's important.

Here's my example.

- **I forgive myself for...**

   i forgive myself for feeling jealous of the love and attention and affection my daughter gets from her dad i forgive myself for thinking he would love me i forgive myself for wanting him to love me

Write away.

- **I forgive myself for...**

_____

_____

_____

_____

_____

_____

_____

_____

_____

_____

_____

_____

_____

_____

_____

_____

_____

_____

_____

_____

_____

_____

_____

_____

Welcome back and good work.

FORGIVING YOUR EX.

Okay, you may not like this step. You need to forgive your ex. Now, I know I said that you need to *forgive* him, but did you hear that you need to *condone* his behavior? No. Absolutely not! <u>Forgiving your ex for whatever the instance does not justify it.</u> Forgiving his actions only helps *you* to move on. You must forgive to move on!

Now, do I think you should say this to him instead of write it for yourself? Not so much. I actually suggest that you do not forgive him to his face and/or in writing. Remember, this book is for *you*, about *you*.

Without forgiveness it is impossible to release resentment!!!

Here's my example.

- **I forgive my ex for…**

    i forgive my ex for knowingly or unknowingly hurting me i forgive my ex for not being the way i want him to be i forgive him for not being who i want him to be

Get that pen out and write.

- **I forgive my ex for…**

_____

_____

_____

_____

_____

_____

_____

_____

_____

_____

_____

_____

_____

_____

_____

_____

_____

_____

_____

_____

_____

_____

_____

_____

Good work. Let's keep going.

Eshida Bissett, a divine, radiant woman who gave me spiritual guidance during this tough time, exposed me to the last part of this exercise.

DECLARE SOMETHING GOOD ABOUT THIS SITUATION OR FEELING.

I had a lot of trouble with this one. How could I possibly come up with something positive from such a hurtful situation? I did and so can you.

Here's my example.

- **Something good about this situation is...**

  i am happy that my daughter has a father who loves her and gives her plenty of affection and attention it is good for her to have both parents in her life

Hello Mr. Ink Pen, meet Mr. Paper.

- **Something good about this situation is...**

_____

_____

_____

_____

Fabulous work! That can be a very tough one but don't you feel good about it?

HAVE YOU EXPRESSED IT ALL?

Since you wrote about all your feelings, I want to make sure that you didn't leave anything out. Are there more things that make you ticked about your ex? What are they? What are you still angry about? Let me see if I can rustle up any irritations for you. Does his incessant lying make you want to scream? Was his cheating unforgivable? Do you want to shake him when he does not believe you? Is he not paying child support on time or at all? Does his child support demand enrage you? Does he change the preplanned schedule at the last minute? Does he not listen to you? Is it infuriating when he doesn't follow through with the promises that he made? Is he a habitual liar? Will he not tell you where he takes your child and you want to know? Does he take your child only to leave them with a sitter the entire visit? Does he criticize your parenting? Is he bad mouthing you to your kids? (God, I hope not.) Get it out. All of it. Take each irritation and follow the previous writing exercises.

For those of you who were raised to keep your emotions and feelings under wraps, this is not the time to play nice or be demure. This is a time to be messy, sloppy, crude, belligerent, angry, sad, or whatever it is that you're feeling. Leave your comfort zone out of this and express what is eating away at you.

I'm going to give you another of my own examples for all the steps thus far so you can see how things can progress using these writing exercises (and it gives you a chance to write some more).

- **Describe what you're feeling**

i hate that my ex fought for more hours in court got them and does NOT take them it pisses me off to change my schedule on a daily basis based on his whim if he wants to see her or not he is so selfish

- **How do you feel about how you feel?**

although i feel justified in being pissed off i hate always being mad at him and then i get mad at myself for wasting so much time and energy on him

- **Forgive yourself**

i forgive myself for letting my life be contingent on what he does or does not do i forgive myself for letting him be the one who controls my emotional state

- **Forgive your ex**

ugh i hate this part i think it's lame but i forgive you for not being in a place in your life where you are capable of taking anyone elses life into consideration

- **Declare something good about the situation**

since i have to say something good the only thing i can think of is i'm glad that my daughter has a dad who wants to see her

Clearly, I was still resistant about doing the last part of the exercise at the time I wrote it but I'm so very grateful now. These exercises truly lead me to a peaceful co-parenting situation. So, if you're resistant, like I was, please keep in mind that three years later, we are still getting along great and it's such a better way to live. Hang in there and keep writing.

- **Describe what you're feeling**

_____

_____

_____

_____

_____

_____

_____

_____

_____

_____

_____

_____

- **How do you feel about how you feel?**

_____

_____

_____

_____

_____

_____

_____

_____

_____

_____

_____

_____

_____

_____

- **Forgive yourself**

_____

_____

_____

_____

_____

_____

_____

_____

_____

_____

_____

_____

_____

- **Forgive your ex**

_____

_____

_____

_____

_____

_____

_____

_____

_____

_____

_____

_____

_____

_____

- **Declare something good about the situation**

_____

_____

_____

_____

_____

_____

_____

_____

_____

_____

_____

_____

Change begins with you. Change ends with you.
Change is your choice.

Chapter 4

Just curious

I'm just curious, when was the last time you hugged your child? When was the last time you and your children laughed together? How long has it been since you said "I love you" to your kids? Make that happen. Put your relationship with your kids before your ex. Put *you* before your relationship with your ex.

TAKE INVENTORY.

Write down the most recent time with your kids that you really had fun with them? Where were you? What were you doing? How long ago was it? Describe the situation.

> - **The last time I had fun with my kids was...**

_____

_____

_____

CREATE JOY FOR YOU AND YOUR CHILD.

Now, I want you to write down how and when you can create a situation like that again in the very near future. If your ex was a part of it, merely leave him out of the equation for your future fun. What can you do to create an enjoyable, playful, stress free activity with your child? Now, I'm not talking about something that *you* enjoy and they do not. This is for the two of you. Could it be as simple as a trip to Chucky E. Cheese? Maybe, it's a camping trip, or an excursion to a theme park. If your child is older, it might be a day of paint ball or go cart racing. Do something fun with them and don't worry about how much it costs. You only go around once and you've got to enjoy the present moment. If you're reading this book, there's a good chance that you've been in a pretty bad place for a while. So, splurge this once. Allow yourself a fantastic time with your child and please make it your personal mission to not say one bad thing about your ex. You don't want to spoil this experience for you or your child.

Jot down some fun ideas and make time for it very soon.

- **My child and I will have a great time doing…**

_____

_____

_____

_____

_____

_____

_____

_____

_____

_____

_____

You. You. You.

I'm curious about something else. When was the last time *you* laughed? When was the last time *you* went out and allowed you a great time? Really, when was it? What was it? Where were you? Was it spontaneous or did you have to plan it? Write about it.

- **The last time I really had a great experience, I was...**

_____

_____

_____

_____

_____

_____

_____

_____

There's a fabulous book, "The Artists Way" written by Julia Cameron. She has you set up an artist's date with yourself once a week. Yes, a date for you and yourself. You choose to do whatever it is that would make you happy. Maybe it's a movie, a trip to the zoo, a manicure and pedicure, a trip to the lake, coloring in a coloring book at a park, knitting, a walk in the rain, a trip to the batting cages, or of course my favorite, a little shopping excursion. Anything goes. Is there something you always want to do and never make time for? Is there something you've always wanted to do for yourself and never created the budget for? Treat yourself. Pamper yourself. Take care of you so that you may take care of your children.

Come up with some ideas that would make you happy, content and relaxed now. Is it a day at the spa? A golf trip you've been wanting to take with your buddies? Is it as simple as making time to go see a movie? Do throwing dinner parties excite you? Does a day alone at the beach or a park with a book sound like heaven? Is it a weekend away while your child is with her dad? Is it merely going to happy hour with friends?

Come up with your dream scenarios and create that experience.

- **The ideal excursion for me is…**

_____

_____

_____

_____

_____

_____

_____

_____

_____

_____

_____

_____

_____

_____

You deserve to be happy just because you exist.

I'm still curious about one more thing, what are your children like? Really, I'm curious what will come to mind as you stop and think about them.

YOUR CHILDREN.

I want you to list all the amazing qualities of your children you can think of for a few reasons. One, I want to remind you of their brilliance and beauty.

Have you ever been in that space where you are doing something and your child calls your name repeatedly and you ignore them, not purposely, mind you, but you've tuned them out because you are so focused on what you are doing that you actually don't hear their voice? Well, I know I have and I know that for me in my height of hating my daughter's father I was so focused on him that I completely lost sight of her. My focus was on the wrong person and I want to bring your attention back to your child.

I also want you to write the fabulous qualities of your child because you very well may realize that some of those qualities actually come from your ex. I know, pish posh him, but come on, it's so much nicer to feel appreciation than hate.

Write away about your little gems.

- **The amazing qualities my child possesses that I appreciate are...**

_____

_____

_____

_____

_____

_____

_____

_____

_____

_____

_____

_____

_____

_____

_____

_____

_____

_____

_____

_____

_____

_____

_____

Okay, now you can make a new list about all the character traits that you would like to change about your child. I.E., they don't behave, they're pushing your buttons on purpose, they are acting out at school, they don't listen... To be honest, my daughter was too young for this list to happen for me but I came up with the idea to make this list while talking with one of my friends who was going through an ugly divorce. Her three boys, who were normally good kids, were acting berserk. She made her list and we came to realize that the kids weren't really acting crazy; they were actually mirroring their parent's behavior. HER behavior! You know that I'm not a fan of the blame game so don't make this list and blame your ex for the things you'd like to change about your child. Make this list and take an honest look at yourself and see if any of your child's negative behavior is a reflection of you. Our children mirror us.

And by the way, after you make this list in particular, I highly recommend tearing this one page out of the book and shredding it. You don't want your child finding this page and reading it for any reason. They are having a hard enough time as it is. This is meant as a tool for you, so be smart about it.

- **Character traits of my child are...**

_____

_____

_____

_____

_____

_____

_____

_____

_____

_____

_____

_____

_____

We can only see beauty in another if we see beauty in ourselves.

Chapter 5

You are not your relationship with your ex

I think that statement is very important to remember so, I'll say it again. You are not your relationship with your ex.

Is there a chance that you have become your relationship? Meaning, are you carrying around the black cloud of your heinous situation with him into your life; your life at work, your life with your child, your life with your friends?

Instead of dismissing those questions, let's start by looking at today. How has your day gone thus far? Did you do a million things for a million people (and share with most of them what your ex has done to you)? Did you do a million things for your boss/employees/clients (and bitch to them about your ex once or twice)? Did you take care of your children (and share too much information about their horrific other parent)? Did you get them fed; bathed, clothed, homework checked and gathered and got them off to school safely (and let your ex effect how you did any of those things)? Did you have some sort of drama with the ex? Did you spend more time enjoying your kids or hating your ex? Did you call and hang up seven times to see if he was in the office "with her"? How much time did you spend yelling at him on the phone? Did you make any time for you? By chance did anyone casually ask you today "How are you?" and you answered with "You're *not* going to believe what *he* did today."

A lot of people in high conflict divorces and/or custody battles don't even realize that when they're asked a question about something innocuous, they turn it into an opportunity to vent their dirty laundry about their ex. Are you one of those people? Really think about your conversations today. What were they about? What are they usually about? Whether or not you think that you do this, become aware of *your* part of conversations. Are you functioning in the present moment, listening and responding? Or are you only half there and fantasizing about your daily drama?

If you do find yourself going on a tangent about his latest antics when it's inappropriate, STOP! Literally, stop. Take a breath and ask yourself, are you going to let him have power over you like that or are you going to take your power back and not buy into the crazy making?

Now, I certainly understand that there will be times that

you will have to call every friend that you have ever had in your entire life to unload and get the support that you need. That's what friends are for (not your kids). I'm just asking you to start taking inventory of how many times a day you rant and rave about your ex. Do you do it to your mutual friends, trying to make them side with you? Do you purposely tell them his latest antics because you know that it will get back to him and you want everyone to know what he did? Are *you* throwing fuel in the fire? You can always go back and do more work in chapter 3 if you need to.

This may sound like I'm changing the subject, but just follow me on this. Many years ago, I had an acting teacher who one day announced that there would be no scene work that day and he instructed us to find a spot on the floor and get comfortable. I did. He dimmed the lights and asked us to close our eyes. He took us through a series of deep breathing exercises and asked us to imagine ourselves at a funeral, our own funeral. Yikes. He said for us to picture all of our friends, family and even enemies there. Now, I don't know about you, but when I truly imagined it, tears sprang to my eyes. I thought he was going to take us on some new age visualization thing, but it turned out to be a very valuable life lesson in awareness. He told us to see specific people, one at a time, and then asked us to listen to what they had to say about us. How did you live your life? More importantly, for this exercise, how did *they* perceive you to live your life?

Try it. Go to a quiet room in your house, close your eyes and really visualize people in your life at your funeral. What would they be saying if they were asked to describe how you lived your life? What would they say filled your days? Would they say that you were you a happy person? Sad? Bitter? Angry? Volatile?

What would *you* think about you? You can be at your own funeral too. Did you appear to be a pretty together person and then fly off the handle on a whim? Did you spend your time loving your children or did you spend your time hating your ex? Did you tell your children that you loved them every day or did you tell your children what a horrible person their other parent was? Did you laugh a lot? Did you yell a lot? Did you fill your time so that you had no time? Were you a victim of the way you saw the world? Was everything being done *to* you? How would you describe you?

Try it.

Did you do the exercise? It can be a pretty powerful experience if you're open to it.

You have the capacity to change your thoughts.
You are capable of making your joy a priority.

Chapter 6

What your hatred is doing to your body

There are articles, studies and entire books devoted to how negative thinking can have a devastating impact on your health. Living with constant negative thoughts about your ex can physically hurt you. Honest. On a side note, "You Can Heal Your Life" by Louise Hay is one of my favorite books about how your negative words and thoughts can create dis-ease.

I believe that she says it best, "Disease is just that, dis-ease." Dis-ease in your mind can wreak havoc on your body causing any number of diseases from constipation to a stiff neck to kidney stones to back problems. The list goes on.

There was a point when I was dealing with so much stress being a new mom, a single new mom, juggling working and living in a constant state of turmoil with my ex that I knew I had to physically get the stress out of my body or I would be doing some serious damage.

My first attempt at dealing with my anxiety and anger was plain and simple, lunges. Yes, leg lunges. Right foot out, lunge all of the way down and stand up again. Left foot out, lunge all of the way down and stand up again. I would stop, drop and lunge anywhere, anytime, anyplace I needed to. Unfortunately, it started to take more than lunges. If I was home and my ex had my daughter and I was riddled with anger by his last phone call or a call from my lawyer regarding our case, I would put on my tennis shoes, grab my cell phone and go for a run. Now, when I say go for a run, I was coming from a place of never exercising, so "a run" really meant a run/walk around the block. Literally. The only good part of being out of shape like that was it didn't take me very long to physically tire myself.

It is so important to rid yourself of draining, wasted, useless anger. I do believe that anger can be used to motivate some out of a bad situation, but for the most part I feel that if anger is not helping you, it is hurting you. Living in anger can eat you away inside.

I had gotten pretty good at letting my anger go through expressing it in writing, venting to a friend or exercising, until my daughter's third Christmas that is. My ex and I had an agreement to share Christmas for the first five years of her life as that holiday is very meaningful to me. Meaningful in a "family" sense, not necessarily in the religious sense. I honestly didn't care where I spent the holiday, or with who as long as I was with my daughter. Well, that Christmas he decided to change the plan and spend the time with her and his girlfriend. Only. Although I was okay with spending it with the three of them, he was not okay with including me. I was truly so devastated by having a toddler, my only child, and not able to spend Christmas with her I broke out in hives. Honest. Hives. Ugh, that was awful and no amount of exercise, writing, shopping, eating, or drinking would change it. I was a walking mess of anxiety and anger. Worst of all, I was embarrassed to talk about it because I knew logically it was just "a day." One of 365 days that *I* decided that I *had* to be with my daughter. A day that *I* put way too much pressure on to be a family day and she was my family.

Now, when I say that I *broke out* in hives, what I really mean is that I *created* those hives.

I had hit a new level of anger that I didn't know how to get through. I remember that I had asked two doctors for an anti depressant and or valium. I couldn't deal. In retrospect, I am now glad that neither of my doctors would prescribe either because it was then that I realized that my anger was my choice. Yep. No matter what the situation was at that moment, I had absolute control over how I felt about the situation. And I felt angry. Very angry. So angry, the anger was literally coming through my skin in a rash. Even my friends were so concerned about me, they had an intervention.

They were tired of my obsession, my anger at my ex.

Now, just because I was aware of the control I had over how I chose to react to things, I had to choose to react differently. The fact that those excruciating days leading up to Christmas had finally passed was very helpful, but the thought of causing a physical ailment in my body actually helped as well. The physical manifestation of my inner turmoil was quite a wakeup call.

I would like to say that that one experience of a physical ailment being caused by my internal mayhem was the first and last, but it wasn't. When my ex was finally given his due 50/50 custody I began having disturbingly bad headaches. So bad in fact, one day I dropped her off and I had to go to the doctor afterwards I was in so much pain. The doctor I saw sent me to the emergency room. The neurologist I saw afterward asked if there was any new stress in my life. No, not that I knew of. It honestly was a mystery to me and him as well since I never had headaches before. A few weeks later, and many more headaches later, I dropped my daughter off again and my head started hurting. It was then that the tears sprang to my eyes and I realized that the headaches began when she started sharing her time equally between our homes. Ugh! I thought I was over letting anything having to do with him affect me. Now, I knew that I didn't like the situation, but I also knew that there was nothing I could do about it and it was good for her to know that her dad wanted her his equal share of time. My friends who were moms at the time said that they envied me, getting time to myself. To that, I always responded with "At least you get to know where your children are and with who 24/7." Not a luxury I had and desperately wanted.

When I realized that the headaches were a manifestation of the new visitation schedule and stress about not knowing the whereabouts of my child for 48 hours at a time, I knew I had to deal with it or continue suffering with debilitating headaches. My first response was to call him and explain my aliment and ask him to please tell me the generic plans of our daughter's activities for her stay with him. "It's your problem, you deal with it." was all I received. Back to the writing work in chapter four for me. I went through the stages of being really pissed, expressing it, forgiving him, forgiving myself, and affirming something good about the situation. Honestly and truly, the headaches went away and never came back. Did I still have moments of really wanting to know where she was? Absolutely. Did I still make the occasional call to try and find out? Absolutely. Did I always get an answer from him? No, but at least it was no longer all consuming. I had to go back to the affirming part of the writing exercise and remind myself that he was very capable and loved her very much.

If you've got any physical aliment, even something as small as a cold sore, I urge you to take a look at it and its potential source and do something about it-mentally, that is. I also highly recommend the book I previously mentioned by Louise Hay, *You Can Heal Your Life.*

Embrace your health. Embrace your life. Embrace your healthy life.

Chapter 7

Parenting and Your Parents

It is nearly impossible to give or accept love in your life when you are living in a place of fear, self loathing and hatred for yourself or for another person. Our children are smarter than we give them credit for. Despite their ages, they pick up on our energies, our moods. Children are very perceptive to hostility and it does affect them. Believe it or not. Like it or not.

What is more important to you, letting your ex know that he is worthless and you think he is a horrible parent, or letting your child know that you are capable of functioning harmoniously with her other parent for her sake and mental well being? Really, it is her mental well being that you are messing with every time you yell at your ex in front of your child or make degrading remarks about him.

At the age of two or at the age of twenty there may come a point during your quarreling that your child will subconsciously believe that your fighting is somehow their fault. Do you really want to put that burden on your child because *you* cannot deal with your own emotions? Do you want your child to grow up believing that she will never get married because marriages never work out and all you do when you get married is fight? Do you want your child to grow up and believe that mommies always hate daddies because they're bad or that all daddies think that mommies are crazy? This may sound extreme, but unless you come from a broken home you may not have any idea of the damage you are potentially inflicting on your children. Children remember. They remember painful situations and you'd be surprised what they will carry with them throughout their adult life.

Your Parents

I told you a little about my parents and you'll hear some more, but, let's look at your life. How did your parents treat each other? Were they loving and kind? Were they vengeful and vindictive? Were they somewhere in the middle, hurling scathing remarks behind closed doors that were not sound proof, then putting on a façade for you and your siblings? Are you repeating your parent's mistakes? Are you doing the very things you swore you would never do to your children? Yes, it is time for inventory.

Get that pen out. Here's an example of mine.

- **Write the first negative thing that comes to your mind about your parents**.

  i hated that mom always said that my dad and every man in the world was a piece of shit and a liar and a cheat and would inevitably leave you and take your money

Whew! Now, you make your list. Don't leave anything out. Remember, anything goes. Your parents are not going to read this. If this process takes days to complete, complete it. (It just occurred to me that your parents may have gotten along fabulously and you don't have one gripe about them. If so, please modify this exercise and do one of two things; write about the first negative experience about any family member that comes to mind or if you aspire to be like you mother/father, list the qualities that you admire. Write about the ways they demonstrated respect for one another. Recall times they were supportive...)

- **Write the first negative thing that comes to your mind about your parents.**

_____

_____

_____

_____

_____

_____

_____

_____

_____

_____

_____

_____

- **And the second.**

- **And the third one**

_____

_____

_____

_____

_____

_____

_____

_____

_____

_____

_____

_____

_____

- **And the forth one.**

Go purchase a separate journal if necessary. Just get it all out.

HOW DO YOU FEEL?

- **Now, how do you feel about what you feel?**

i feel bad that i feel like my mom was pathetic

Your turn.

- **How do you feel about how you feel?**

_____

_____

_____

_____

_____

_____

_____

After writing that, I wanted to get to the next part as quickly as possible.

FORGIVE YOURSELF.

- **Forgive yourself for feeling what you feel.**

i forgive myself for thinking my mom was pathetic

Have at it.

- **Forgive yourself for feeling what you feel.**

_____

_____

_____

_____

_____

_____

_____

I just realized that *my* mom may actually read this one day so I'd like to make something clear to her and to you; this is not the blame game. I'm not blaming my mom for my previous bad relationships with men (although I did until I realized it was MY responsibility and MY choice to create the kind of relationship I wanted). I am merely acknowledging my truth as I remember it so that I may let it go. I know that I am an adult and that I am responsible for thinking my own thoughts. Only I control what tapes run through my head. If I choose to hear her voice over and over about how bad men are, that is my doing. Not hers. I can actively choose to reprogram those tapes with something positive about men so that I may expect to be met with a positive relationship instead of attracting a negative one.

Moving on. Forgive your parents. Again, you are not condoning what they did; you are forgiving them for it. I'd imagine that if you had all the details of their lives that led them to do or say whatever they did to you, you'd realize that they probably did the best they could with where they were at. I repeat I'm not condoning their actions; I'm trying to make it easier for you to forgive them.

Forgive Your Parents

- **Forgive your parents.**

i forgive you mom for not realizing the damaging impact you would have on my adult life because you were screwed up about men and made the wrong choices for yourself

- **Forgive your parents.**

_____

_____

_____

_____

_____

_____

_____

_____

_____

And yes, now we must –

FIND SOMETHING POSITIVE ABOUT THE SITUATION.

If you find yourself holding your pen that just won't write, I understand. You may be staring at a blank page for a very long time, but please do not skip this step.

My example.

- **Declare something good about the situation.**

   i am glad that i now know that i am not predestined to re-live my mothers life that i can create something new by thinking something new and choosing my own type of man

- **Declare something good about the situation.**

_____

_____

_____

Stopping a negative cycle in your family does not just happen. *You* have to make it happen.

YOUR PARENTS AFFECTED YOU AND YOU'RE AFFECTING YOUR CHILDREN.

I have a girlfriend whose father abused her growing up. Come to find out that her father was abused and for the love of Pete, she's dating an abusive man who recently broke her arm! It's mind blowing as an outsider to see the cycle. It's also obvious as an outsider to see the cycle. I do understand that it's not so easy to see when you are actually in it. That is why we're doing this work.

How did your parents deal with their anger?

- **Write the first words that come to mind to describe your parents.**

My list looked something like this…

Stupid
Immature
Childish
Pathetic
Absurd

- **Write the first words that come to mind to describe your parents.**

_____

_____

_____

_____

_____

_____

_____

_____

_____

_____

_____

_____

You know what comes next.

- **Write your uncensored feelings about the situation.**

_____

_____

_____

_____

_____

_____

_____

_____

_____

_____

_____

_____

- **Write how you feel about how you feel.**

_____

_____

_____

_____

_____

_____

_____

_____

_____

_____

_____

_____

- **Forgive yourself for how you feel.**

_____

_____

_____

_____

_____

_____

_____

_____

_____

_____

_____

_____

_____

- **Forgive your parents.**

_____

_____

_____

_____

_____

_____

_____

_____

_____

_____

_____

_____

- **Declare something good about the situation.**

_____

_____

_____

_____

_____

_____

_____

_____

_____

_____

_____

_____

Now that you've identified how your parents dealt with their anger toward each other, how do *you* deal with your anger at your ex?

Do you hurl slanderous remarks at your ex in front of your child? Do you make derogatory remarks about your ex to others in front of your child? Do you make him look less than anything short of a loving parent in front of your child? Do you tell your child that you cannot afford something that she wants because her dad is not paying child support? Do you blame your child's problems on your ex? If any of these questions are ringing any bells, please for the love of your child, STOP IMMEDIATLY! You are an adult. You are capable of making your own choices. You can choose over and over (and over and over again if need be) to be the bigger person for your child's sake. In each and every moment, no matter what terrible, pathetic thing he has done now, you can choose to <u>react</u> differently. It can be an arduous task, and it is not in any way, shape or form justifying his actions; it is merely a way to take care of yourself and your children. You and they are the priority. Let them know that - by *your* actions, reactions and behaviors.

I have a friend who is one of the most well-adjusted people I know and she has parents who went through an ugly divorce as well. Despite the fact that she is over thirty years old and her parents have been divorced for well over twenty years, she is still afraid to marry her live-in boyfriend of eleven years because she knows her parents will not be in the same room together. Who will she invite to the wedding? Her mom? Her dad? If she invites them both, will there be a fight? Will her dad bring his girlfriend? Will it make her mom sad? What if her mom doesn't have someone to bring? The internal conflict *still* goes on and on with her. Twenty years later!!! It's crazy! And to this day, her parents still lobby for her to spend holidays with them by outdoing the other parent's festivities. It is ludicrous. You have no idea the potential long term damage you are causing by openly fighting with your ex in front of your child.

Let's apply my friend's predicament to a child, or even a teen in high school. Assuming they are aware of your hatred and fighting and they have a softball game, a dance concert, a spelling bee…whatever, and it's only their dad's day. Imagine how potentially difficult and/or stressful for them to either invite their mother or be worried about what may happen if they both show up. It's just not fair to the kids!

You are a fantastic role model.   Peace be with you.
May peace be with them.

Chapter 8

When your ex takes on a new partner

WHEN IT HAPPENED TO ME.

Ah, the agonizing misery. I remember the pain as if it just happened yesterday. I assumed it was coming because my ex frequently had fresh baked cookies at his house and clearly he did not make them.

At first I thought, "Oh, there's someone else in the picture. Well, at least she makes good cookies." I even told him to tell her that he liked chocolate chocolate chip so I could enjoy one of my favorites.

It was easy to dismiss the idea of him having a girlfriend until I met her. She was real. Really attractive and really in his life. Ugh! It hit me like a ton of bricks and I couldn't figure out how I could be so easily devastated by the situation. I suppressed it for about two days until I went to drop my daughter off and she was there. I was friendly, casual and appeared comfortable with the situation. The key word in that last sentence was "appeared." I was about to send my daughter off on an adventure to Santa Barbara with my ex and his new woman. (Insert tears here.)

So, I handled it like any other rational, level headed female would. I stopped at my local drug store, picked up a box of hair color, went home, colored and cut my hair, went to lunch with a friend, proceeded to hit my favorite department store for a pair of shoes, came home, went for a jog, cried and pouted like a five year old for a few hours, then I ate ice-cream. A lot of ice-cream.

As the days went by I thought I was over it until she turned up at a barbeque that was supposed to be "family time". It was then that I realized I needed to really work through the situation instead of finding distractions, although I did enjoy my new hair style.

I went to the computer and worked through the whole identifying / forgiving steps that we did earlier and I realized something very important. I will share my revelation with you and how I got there.

- **My uncensored feelings about the situation.**

  i hate that my ex has a new girlfriend and that she is so pretty he is just going to dump her when he realizes that she is not his mother and that no one will ever be and she is probably just the "fly by nighter" that he said she was unless he lied about that since he lies about everything else i'm sad i'm jealous i'm mad i'm hurt

- **How I felt about how I felt.**

i feel like a stupid dumb little girl who has not grown up

- **Forgive myself for how I feel.**

i forgive myself for feeling stupid feelings that are not controllable and it is okay for me to feel how ever i do whether or not it seems appropriate or inappropriate i forgive myself for being affected by his actions

- **Forgive my ex.**

i forgive you for not loving me i forgive you for not wanting to be in a relationship with me

- **Declare something good about the situation.**

Well, this is the part I could not come up with. I stared at the page for what seemed like an hour and I reread what I had written over and over hoping that it would trigger something for me. Anything.

As I read "*i feel like a stupid dumb little girl who has not grown up*" for the hundredth time, I pictured myself as a young girl and I saw a stupid, dumb, but cute, little girl. I didn't know why I was picturing myself as dumb when I was little, but I was feeling that way. Why was I dumb? Why would I think I was stupid at such a young age? And it all clicked for me in that moment. I really didn't want my ex to be my partner in life; I was only trying to win him over, just like I did with my father.

As a child, my father never gave me appropriate attention or affection, as my ex never did when we were dating. As a child I was always in quest of something I could do to get my dad's undivided attention so that he would love me, or at least tell me that he did.

While dating my ex, he could not even use the word "dating" or "girlfriend" even though we spent a great deal of time together and were clearly "dating." Despite the fact that his closest friends had told me that he was in love with me and that they had never seen him like this, my ex was not capable of verbalizing or admitting his fondness for me on that level (I thought he was just scared that he was in love and would come around. Sometimes my happy bubble gets foggy and I can't see very clearly). The closest I ever got from my ex saying that we were dating was once when he told me something to the effect of "I have never had as much fun with someone as I have with you." My dad never said "I love you" and my ex never said "I love you". I was trying to win. If I could win over my ex, I would somehow be conquering one of my childhood struggles I had with my dad.

I had realized that I had lost. I was never going to get what I wanted from my ex and seeing his new girlfriend reminded me of that yet again. Sometimes admitting and acknowledging where we are and how we got there can be painful, devastating, uncomfortable and lonely. On a positive note, it leads me to the last step.

- **Declare something good about the situation.**

i now see the pattern i have recreated in order to heal a wounded piece of myself i am willing to change it and i can and i will

I also went back and forgave my father for not being capable of giving or showing love to me appropriately. I cried for the next two days mourning my past and accepting my present. I had no idea that there was so much sadness about both situations to be expressed and healed.

In all of my self help reading over the years I have realized that we, collectively, like to live in our comfort zones even when they are not so comfortable. It's what we know. I have come out of this experience ahead of the game because there can be no change without awareness and I can't tell you how good it feels to live in the land of love vs. the world of fear.

BACK TO YOU.

So, does your ex have a new partner? Have you met her? Were/are you devastated? Do you question your children about her incessantly? Does a swear word slip out of your mouth when you mention her name? Do you make your child feel guilty for liking her? Do you bad mouth her whenever possible? Do you bad mouth your ex for being with her? Do you drive your child around in your car and follow them? Oh, wait! That was my mom. (Yes, I also did the writing exercises about this as well.)

I know a woman who is about to go to court for custody/child support issues and her kids literally go back and forth every other day but have two days in a row with her. So it's a 4/3 day schedule as of now. Although she is getting enough support to cover all her residential and living expenses, she told her kids that if her dad got that one more day of custody and make it an even 50/50 split (which he is trying to do) she would get less support and they'd have to pick up and move 400 miles away from their dad, both sets of grandparents, their school, friends, social activities... Now, if she's doing this just because she's mad that her ex has moved in with his girlfriend or she's using the kids to send a message (or threat) to their father, or she's just living in fear (and should talk to a therapist instead of the kids), the kids are terrified and panicked they will have to move. Does this sound like a scorned woman who is putting her kids in the middle? What do you sound like?

What is most important here, the mental welfare of your children or the temporary fix of vindictiveness because *you* are miserable, angry, jealous and/or lonely?

Take care of yourself; deal with whatever feelings you may be experiencing as your ex takes on a new relationship. I promise you this; the intensity of your discomfort with the situation will pass at some point. IF YOU ALLOW IT. If you're all consumed with your feelings, that's okay too. Accept them. Get them out. Talk to a professional (not your kids), unload on your friends (not your kids), write about it until your hand cramps up, exercise them out, just do something! Cry your way through them. Eventually, you'll just feel exhausted, like a hollow pit and a feeling of tremendous relief will follow.

Have at it.

- **Describe what you're feeling.**

_____

_____

_____

_____

_____

_____

_____

_____

_____

_____

_____

_____

_____

- **How do you feel about how you feel?**

_____

_____

_____

_____

_____

_____

_____

_____

_____

_____

_____

_____

_____

- **Forgive yourself.**

_____

_____

_____

_____

_____

_____

_____

_____

_____

_____

_____

_____

_____

- **Forgive your ex.**

_____

_____

_____

_____

_____

_____

_____

_____

_____

_____

_____

_____

_____

_____

- **Declare something good about the situation.**

_____

_____

_____

_____

_____

_____

_____

_____

_____

_____

_____

_____

You owe it to yourself to do something constructive with your feelings besides stuffing them. At some point your body will reject those attempts and you will combust. It may transpire in lashing out verbally and irrationally, or it may be acting out inappropriately, or your body may just force you to stop suppressing by creating some sort of dis-ease. Well, you know, you read chapter 7.

It *can be* difficult, but it *is* a choice and it is possible. I believe that you are strong enough to get through it. Through it, and over it. Look how far you have come in your life. Look at the adversities you have surpassed.

You are worthy of happiness. You will get through this. I believe in you.

Chapter 9

Do Not Mistake Your Kindness for Weakness

Remember when I said there would be a lot of writing on your part? Well, this is a going to be a different kind of writing, documenting.

I know that we've been working on forgiving your ex, forgiving yourself and functioning from a new more grounded, more aware, more stable, more loving place, but let's not lose sight of reality. A brilliant acting teacher of mine, Leigh Kilton Smith, always said, "Do not mistake my kindness for weakness." Now, I will say it to you, "Do not mistake **your** kindness for weakness!" There are still legal matters at hand including custody and child support. If they are not currently issues up for debate, it doesn't mean that they won't be in the future and you need to be fully prepared for whatever comes your way.

If you're thinking that everything is fine in those arenas, it doesn't mean that it always will be. He may take you to court to revisit those issues or you may be the one filing to amend the current situation. You never know. Prepare so that you do not have to re-pair in the future causing an inordinate amount of potential grief, frustration, and money.

Document everything. Everything. I don't care how simple or silly you think it is, document it. Save all of the e-mails that are exchanged. Save all of the letters that are exchanged. Log the child support he sends and when he sent it. Was it on time? Was it late? How late? Log the hours that he takes. Log the hours that you offered. Log the days and times he takes her. Does he or has he yelled at you in front of her? God forbid, has he hit you, threatened to hit you? Worse? Document it.

This is not a chapter to skim over because the two of you are getting along right now or you're talking about getting back together or you don't think you have a reason to do this. I will say it again, you never know. I'm not saying for you to panic and try and retrace every moment from your separation to the present, but if there are significant events that you can recall the date and the event, write them down. Did he promise to take her and her friends to Disneyland on her birthday and he never showed up? Did he not take her when he was supposed to for a weekend because he didn't feel like it? Has he ever been intoxicated when he came to pick her up? Has he forgotten to pick her up from school?

Document it all and every few months give an updated copy to a trusted friend or family member just in case. Just in case your computer goes on the fritz, just in case you lose your journal, just in case, who knows what, just do it to be safe.

<u>I don't want your mind to take you to a defensive place when you document</u>. You are not preparing for an attack, you are merely taking care of you and your child by having important facts on hand if need be. There is a possibility that this information could help your child as well. For example, if your child started to have problems in school or starting acting out, you could go back to your log of visitation and examine the possibilities. Have the days changed? Have the hours been extended or decreased at all? I don't even mean significantly, sometimes an hour or two can affect them. Has there been a switch in days? Has she started a new school? Did you always pick her up after school and now he is? Kids need and like schedule and routine. It makes them feel in control of their world.

Do not share any of this documentation with your child. I repeat, do not share this information with your child. It is not to be used as a tool to drive her from the other parent. It is not a dirty laundry list to regurgitate to her when she tells you that she wants to spend time with the ex. You are an adult, act like one.

You are smart enough and capable enough to take care of yourself and your child.

Chapter 10

You Want Me to What?

I want you to be open to the idea of setting up a "shared visit" with your child and your ex. Yes, a visit where you, your ex and your child are all in the same location at the same time, on purpose. Before you dismiss the idea, please continue to read this chapter. This is not meant as a torture session for any of you. This is not meant as a place for fighting, nasty glares, biting sarcasm, a verbal boxing ring or a place to rehash unresolved issues. Will you possibly feel that way at times? It's possible. Are you a mature, responsible parent who chooses to put their child's emotional well-being first? I believe that you are.

A shared visit day is meant for your child. Can you imagine how good that would feel for a child to have their two parents together again if only for a short time (and get along)? They will never have their mother and father living in the same household again. Why not give them the sense of security that neither parent is going to abandon them? Show them that you are both capable of putting your personal feelings aside and demonstrate how two grown-ups can behave. You made this child together and for the rest of her life, you two, together, will be her parents, her only biological parents. If she knows now that you both can share her maturely, it will make her life a lot easier.

Imagine this…you and your ex are separated. You haven't had a shared visit day and it's your child's dance recital, baseball game, school play… Might they be anxious about how their parents will relate? Possibly fight? Think that one of you will have hurt feelings if they have more interaction with the other parent? They do think about these things. They may not discuss it or even be aware of why they feel uneasy, but they just may.

If your child is under the age of five, I would suggest one shared visit every two weeks or at least one a month. If she is over six, I would suggest at least once a month. It could be done as she goes from one house to the next. It could, and should be on neutral territory. You could meet at a restaurant (alternating who picks up the tab), the park, the mall, a theme park (there are a lot of distractions there), after her soccer game, before her dance recital.

I would encourage you to enlist in the support of your new husband / wife or your boyfriend / girlfriend in this endeavor. If you must bring them along, then make sure that they will be pleasant from beginning to end.

Are you thinking that this seems impossible? Well, then, I want you to rethink it, only this time, think about it from your child's perspective. If you can't fathom the idea of being amiable for an hour or so, I'd like to introduce you to the phrase "Fake it 'till you make it."

Let me be very clear about something, if you or your child were in an abusive relationship with your ex, this is not for you! If that in fact was the case, my hope for you is that you are seeking help with a licensed therapist and very skilled legal counsel in this matter. Do not put yourself or your child in a precarious situation.

As you answer these next few questions, I'd like to remind you to put your pen to the page and write your stream of conscious thoughts. Stop writing only when you are finished. You may find that some of your fears are just that, **F**alse **E**xpectations **A**ppearing **R**eal.

Let's look at a few things…

- **Is it possible to act "as if" you got along with your ex? If not, why? Is it something you can change? If so, how?**

_____

_____

_____

_____

_____

_____

_____

_____

_____

_____

_____

- **Could you handle yourself appropriately for an hour or so with your ex? What derogatory remark may slip out?** I'd like to give you this opportunity to vent. On the page, people. On the page.

_____

_____

_____

_____

_____

_____

_____

_____

_____

_____

_____

- **What is the worst case scenario if I set up a "shared visit" with my ex?**

_____

_____

_____

_____

_____

_____

_____

_____

_____

_____

_____

_____

- **How could *you* make this work?**

_____

_____

_____

_____

_____

_____

_____

_____

_____

_____

_____

_____

_____

- **How would you ask him? What would you say?**

_____

_____

_____

_____

_____

_____

_____

_____

_____

_____

_____

Now, go back, and as an outsider, objectively read what you just wrote about how you would ask him. Did you use sarcasm? Did you pose it as a demand or as a request? Were you cold and bitter? Did you make it sound like it was something you'd rather live without and you'd rather he did not acquiesce to your suggestion? Did you demand the time and place or did you make suggestions as to what could possibly work for both of you? Did you tell him to leave his new woman at home, or say that you prefer if it was just the three of you, but if he felt more comfortable to bring her, then that would be okay too?

- **How could you ask him differently, in a way that he may be receptive?**

_____

_____

_____

_____

_____

_____

_____

- **How would a shared visit benefit your child?**

_____

_____

_____

_____

_____

_____

_____

_____

_____

_____

_____

_____

You *are* capable of rising above the situation for one short hour every two weeks (or month). I know that you are.

SUGGESTIONS FOR A PLEASANT SHARED VISIT DAY:

:When conversing with the ex, keep the topic to matters that relate to your child ONLY.

:Do not discuss the past.

:Do not ask questions about his personal life, nor volunteer information about yours.

:Do not discuss money, child support or otherwise.

:Do not discuss any legal matters between the two of you.

:If you start to feel the desire to scream obscenities, make a trip to the bathroom and breathe (lunges also work well.)

:If you suddenly cannot stomach another minute, avoid looking at your ex. Keep eye contact with your child. Looking at her will remind you of what is important.

:If your ex becomes abusive or inappropriate, have a graceful exit strategy planned.

:Choose an ending time before you set up the meeting.

:Prepare your child who she is going to leave with so there's no drama or hurt feelings.

:End with a generic pleasantry. "Have a good day." works just fine.

A shared visit day is not the only thing I want you to do. I'd like you to occasionally converse with your ex about your child's day to day life. Depending on the age of your child that will mean different things. If your child is a toddler, you can ask your ex about her napping schedule, her bed time, are her baths at night or in the morning, what or how she ate that day. If they are older you can ask him how she is with doing homework at his house or who her friends are or if she arrives there after school on time. Maybe I can explain the purpose of this best through two short stories a child psychologist, Lori, relayed to me.

Lori was working with a couple who was divorced and never spoke, yet they shared equal custody of their twelve year old daughter, I'll call her, Maggie. The couple brought their daughter to Lori because they were baffled by her behavior. Maggie had been enrolled in an after school activity for the entire year. When the time came to re-sign up for the activity, the teacher called and wanted to make sure that Maggie would not be dropping out again as she did the prior year. As you can imagine her parents were both flabbergasted to find out that their daughter had not been where she was supposed to be for the last year. Maggie's response was that if her mom didn't know what she did or where she went while she was at her dad's house, and her dad didn't know what she did or where she went while at her mom's house, why couldn't she do what she wanted to do since neither of them care what she does.

This couple had so much hatred toward one another that they couldn't even talk to their daughter about what she did when she was with the other parent because they did not want to hear about their ex. Somewhere along the way these parents forgot that they were co-parenting.

Lori was also seeing a little boy who was five, Billy, and his parents who had been divorced almost two years. Billy had been having trouble in school and they were trying to get to the root of it. One session Lori asked his mom what his favorite color was and his mom said, blue. His dad then interjected, "No, his favorite color is red." When Lori asked Billy what his favorite color was, he stared at her and started to cry. He didn't know how to answer. Come to find out that Billy had a different favorite everything depending on whose house he was in. He had different routines in each house, neither of them remotely similar to each other; a different bed time, a different lunch box, different best friends, he even liked different foods. Billy was so confused about where he would be on what night that to help him keep track, he wore his underpants backward if he was at daddy's and the right way at mommy's.

Billy's parents had no idea how difficult it was for him to literally be shuttled back and forth day after day, night after night without ANY communication.

Now, I certainly know parents who are the extreme opposite and grill their poor children about any information regarding their ex. How are your communication skills with your ex regarding your child? Could you do better? Will you do better? I believe that you will try.

SUGGESTIONS FOR A PLEASANT, YET INFORMATIVE, CONVERSATION REGARDING YOUR CHILD:

:Stick to the topic at hand.

:Communicate via e-mail if you are unable to do

it in person or over the phone.

:Don't tell him that he is doing something wrong.

:If you have a request for him to do something another way, make it a request, not a demand.

:Keep the topic to matters that relate to your child ONLY.

:Do not discuss the past.

:Do not ask questions about his personal life, nor volunteer information about yours.

:Do not discuss money, child support, new love interest, old love interests, rumors, manners, gossip, gripes…in these conversations.

:Do not discuss any legal matters between the two of you.

:If you start to feel the desire to scream obscenities, tell him you need to call him back at a later time.

:End with a generic pleasantry. "Thank you." works just fine.

You are stronger than your circumstance. You are capable of rising high. You are brave enough to be the one who raises the bar and most importantly, your child will be the better for it.

Chapter 11

Are you a statistic?

I'd like to share with you some staggering statistics I found while researching for this book. Constance Ahrons's book, "The Good Divorce" states that just twelve percent of divorced parents are able to create friendly, low-conflict relationships after divorce. Twelve!

In one study Judith Wallerstein, author of "Second Chances", conducted on couples divorced for ten years reported that *half* the women were still very angry with their ex-spouse. Half! Fifty percent! What a terrible way to spend ten years of your life and think of all of those children that are affected.

If you're thinking that *your* child has no idea that you despise your ex, you're wrong. If you think that she doesn't sense your anger, you're wrong. If you think she cannot see you grit your teeth when you speak to him, you're wrong. You really need to take a close look at what you are teaching her by your example. I'm not saying for you to be a people pleaser and a doormat, letting him walk all over you. That is not a great lesson either. I'm saying take care of your issues with him on your own. If need be, converse with him on your own time, out of earshot of your child. Use a therapist's office as a place to converse if necessary. There was a time that my ex and I used to see a child psychologist together about once a month to air our grievances that we could not see eye to eye on and basically make sure that we were doing the best for our child that we possibly could.

Here's a statistic I found interesting yet disturbing. "A study conducted at the University of Washington divided 117 households into three categories: "martially distressed", "martially supported", and "unmarried mothers," and found that children of the families that had marital distress had significantly higher disciplinary problems than children from families that reported a happy marriage, but those children of unmarried mothers had a considerably higher amount of disciplinary problems than those who were from the other two categories." Carolyn Webster Stratton, "Marital Support," 417-430. Cited on page 106 of _The Abolition of Marriage,_ by MaggieGallagher

I don't know about you, but reading something like this makes me even more determined not to let my daughter become a statistic in this category. Where do you fall in this study? How are *your* children doing? Do you blame your ex for their school troubles, their inadequate social skills, and their bad attitude? Remember, the blame game does not exist here. What are *you* possibly doing to contribute to their disciplinary problems? More importantly, what could you do to help them? Are you encouraging or impatient? Do you find the good in what they have done or do you point out the bad? Do you give positive reinforcement or demand more? How do you wake them up in the morning, with a "Good morning, let's get going." or "God damn it, Sarah, would you get up when your alarm goes off? You're starting to piss me off."

How do you speak to your children when you are angry with them? Do you talk to them like you do your ex? Are your questions accusatory, judgmental, and not really questions at all? Is it just another way for you to unload your anger inappropriately? How would you tell your child that it's time to go to your ex's house? A. "Time to get ready for your dad's house." B. "Get your shit together. You're going to be late to your dad's house and I don't want to hear him bitch at me for it." It sounds extreme, but I've heard it from parents who don't even realize they are spewing hatred to the detriment of their child.

I was recently with a nine year old girl whose parents are getting a divorce and she said to me, "My mom said that if I knew who my dad really was, it'd scare the shit outta me." That poor kid was so confused about what that statement meant, where it came from, what her dad really did or didn't do to make her mom say that, if her mom was trying to get her to be scared of her dad, if she would get in trouble for repeating it and the list went on. When the mother was confronted about it, the response was, "It was taken out of context." True or not true, the mom still said it and it still freaked the kid out. That was just *one* statement. Imagine what days filled with bitching about your ex can do to your child.

Hopefully by this point in the book you have worked through a great deal of your anger toward your ex. Let's take a closer look and see if there are other areas that need to be uncovered, expressed, written and released.

Are you harboring ill will toward your ex that you have not expressed to him, a friend, a therapist, or even yourself? Does he make a certain face or have a specific mannerism that really gets your goad? Does the sound of his voice make your skin crawl? Does hearing your child say that she loves him irritate you because she does not know what an ass he is to you? You tell me. What have you not expressed that you need to?

Don't be a statistic. You have the tools you need right in front of you, so use them. I'll remind you in case you need a quick reference.

- Write your uncensored feelings about the situation.
- Write how you feel about how you feel.
- Forgive yourself for how you feel.
- Forgive your ex.
- Declare something good about the situation.

I'm proud of you for taking action. I'm proud of
you for choosing to move through your
circumstance into a better one. I'm proud of you for
being you!

Chapter 12

In Closing

I have gone through the emotional wringer dealing with my past and accepting my present so that I could create a new future. It has been at times unbelievably overwhelming, sad, painful and lonely.

Who knows, maybe all of this has happened so that I may help *you* get through your challenging situation. As you close the last page of this book, I'd like to say thank you for going on my journey with me. I hope that I have helped you.

I hope that you are walking away from your past negative experience and turning it into a positive one.

I also hope that your past relationship with your ex does not prevent you from having future relationships.

I hope that you are co-parenting in peace and harmony with oodles of love for your child.

On Risk

To laugh is to risk appearing the fool.
To weep is to risk appearing sentimental.
To reach out to another is to
risk exposing your true self.
To place your ideas, your dreams before the crowd
is to risk their loss.
To love is to risk not being loved in return.
To live is to risk dying.
To hope is to risk despair.
To try is to risk failure.
But risks must be taken, because the greatest hazard
in life is to risk waiting.
The person who risks nothing, does nothing, has
nothing and is nothing.
He avoids suffering and sorrow.
But he simply cannot learn, feel, change, love or live.
He has forfeited freedom.
Only a person who risks is free.

Unknown

Now, go play with your kids!

36011280R00093

Made in the USA
San Bernardino, CA
10 July 2016